50p

(44)

G000045062

Butterflies

RUNNING PRESS
PHILADELPHIA · LONDON

A Running Press® Miniature Edition™
© 2000 by Running Press
All rights reserved under the Pan-American
and International Copyright Conventions
Printed in China

Library of Congress Cataloging-in-Publication Number 99-74345

ISBN 0-7624-0757-3

This book may be ordered by mail from the publisher. Please
include $1.00 for postage and handling.
But try your bookstore first!

Running Press Book Publishers
125 South Twenty-second Street
Philadelphia, Pennsylvania 19103-4399

Visit us on the web!
www.runningpress.com

INTRODUCTION

What has the weight of a leaf, the colors of a rainbow, the speed of a bird, and tastes with its feet? The answer could only be a butterfly. These delicate insects have long been appreciated by biologists, artists, and writers. The love of nature has been inspired in many people by these varied, beautiful creatures.

Butterflies transform static landscapes into scenes of vibrant motion and color. Almost every field, forest, or dune has butterflies floating near its treetops or close to the ground. Gathered at puddles on country roads after rains, parties of tiger swallowtail and sulphur butterflies will explode into clouds of yellow, black, and white wings as you pass them. In Mexico, masses of orange and black monarchs blanket pine trees and goldenrod during their annual migrations from the U.S. Butterflies give us joy and beauty wherever they alight.

Though a butterfly's array of colors adds to the beauty of our land, the patterns found on its wings were not created for our pleasure. Rather, these designs are critical to a butterfly's survival. The orange and black of the monarch warn birds of this butterfly's sickening taste. The trailing wingtips of the swallowtail and the eyespots on the wings of the wood satyr divert predators from more vital body parts. The mottled coloring of the anglewing's sharply-cut wings provides excellent camouflage.

Few organisms have such dramatic life cycles as these creatures. They grow quickly from tiny eggs, often no bigger than the periods on this page, to hungry multi-legged caterpillars. Then they wrap themselves in chrysalises to complete their startling transformations into winged adults. For most butterflies, this change allows them to find mates and exploit new sources of food. Despite its utter practicality, humans find butterfly metamorphosis to be one of the great miracles of nature.

Butterfly bodies are superbly designed machines—light and agile enough to ride breezes and evade predators, yet strong enough to withstand the buffeting of strong winds. The adults of some species are capable of flights of hundreds of miles. Butterflies depend on high-energy flower nectar for food. In return, the butterflies pollinate the flowers as they move from one to another.

With a little practice, it is easy to observe the intricate relationships between butterflies and plants. Lilac, buddleia, boneset, butterfly weed, sedum, ageratum, lavender, daisy, and delphinium attract the adults of many species. Caterpillars often feast upon specific species. Maintaining the health and diversity of these plants ensures a population of butterflies year after year.

This book presents the most vibrant and visible butterfly species found in North America, as well as thoughts from butterfly lovers as to why these creatures hold our imaginations.

Butterflies

There is as much to be discovered and to astonish in magnifying an insect as a star.

Thaddeus William Harris (1795–1856)
American entomologist

The first butterflies probably evolved 80 to 100 million years ago, and diversified into the modern families long before the oldest known butterfly fossils formed, about 48 million years ago.

...I knew the birds
and insects, which looked
fathered by the
flowers...
butterflies, that bear
Upon their blue wings such
red embers round
They seem to scorch the blue
air into holes
Each flight they take...

Elizabeth Barrett Browning
(1806–1861)
English poet

CALIFORNIA HAIRSTREAK
Satyrium californica

Found in hill country and mountains west of the Rocky Mountains.

ORANGE SULPHUR
Colias eurytheme

Common in meadows across the continent; adults visit legumes, clover, and alfalfa and gather at mud puddles.

NORTHERN
CHECKERSPOT
Charidryas palla

♀

♂

Inhabits woodlands in the Northwest. Adults often congregate at puddles during the summer.

CLODIUS PARNASSIAN
Parnassius clodius

This relative of the swallowtails lives in Rocky Mountain woodlands.

SPICEBUSH SWALLOWTAIL
Pterourus troilus

This large eastern swallowtail drinks the nectar of lilac, honeysuckle, and spicebush flowers.

Variety's the spice of life
That gives it all its flavour.

William Cowper (1731–1800)
English poet

Literature and butterflies are the two sweetest passions known to man.

Vladimir Nabokov (1899–1977)
Russian-born American novelist

There are approximately 20,000 known species of butterflies. Untold thousands of undiscovered species probably occupy the rainforests that ring the earth's equator.

I found it to be as I expected, a perfectly new and most magnificent species, and one of the most gorgeously colored butterflies in the world.... The beauty and brilliancy of this insect are indescribable, and none but a naturalist can understand the intense excitement I experienced.... My heart began to beat violently, the blood rushed to my head, and I felt much

more like fainting than I have done when in apprehension of immediate death. I had a headache the rest of the day, so great was the excitement....

Alfred Russel Wallace (1823–1913)
English naturalist
Upon discovering the birdwing, the largest known butterfly, in Malaysia

ANICIA
CHECKERSPOT
Occidryas anicia

*Sometimes known as the
"Paintbrush Checkerspot," this
butterfly inhabits meadows and
other grassy areas in the Rocky
Mountain region.*

HACKBERRY
BUTTERFLY
Asterocampa celtis

This strong flier occupies eastern and midwestern woods, especially near its namesake plant.

DOGFACE BUTTERFLY
Zerene cesonia

An adaptable species that occupies diverse habitats, ranging from woods to deserts to prairies across the midwest and southern U.S.

SARA ORANGETIP
Anthocharis sara

The Sara Orangetip inhabits the West Coast from California to Alaska. Females with yellow wingtips have been recorded.

VARIEGATED FRITILLARY
Euptoieta claudia

Living in all except the most heavily wooded areas, this butterfly is especially attracted to the passion flower.

The beautiful rests on the foundations of the necessary.

Ralph Waldo Emerson (1803–1882)
American essayist and poet

The beauty of a butterfly's wing, the beauty of all things, is not a slave to purpose, a drudge sold to futurity. It is excresence, superabundance, random ebullience, and sheer waste to be enjoyed in its own high regard.

Donald Culross Peattie (1898–1964)
American naturalist and writer

The patterns of butterflies' wings, once regarded with merely interested admiration, have become...the pages on which we can read the past history of the everlasting conflict between the hunter and the hunted, and the complicated process by which new forms have adapted themselves to changed and changing circumstances.

Harry Eltringham
Nineteenth-century Irish-born
English entomologist

Colors speak all languages.

Joseph Addison (1672–1719)
English essayist and statesman

Some butterflies have bold wing patterns that can be perceived only in the ultraviolet portion of the spectrum. These patterns help butterflies of related species, such as the various sulphur butterflies, tell each other apart during mating.

RED ADMIRAL
Vanessa atalanta

Inhabits the edges of woodlands throughout North America. The caterpillars feed on hops and nettles.

AMERICAN COPPER
Lycaena phlaeas

Occupies areas of new growth and open space in the upper U.S. and lower Canada.

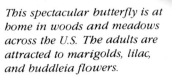

TIGER SWALLOWTAIL
Pterourus glaucus

This spectacular butterfly is at home in woods and meadows across the U.S. The adults are attracted to marigolds, lilac, and buddleia flowers.

BALTIMORE
Euphydryas phaeton

Lives in moist, wooded areas in the eastern U.S. The adults are attracted to foxglove, ash, turtlehead, and plantain.

ZEPHYR
ANGLEWING
Polygonia zephyrus

A strong flier, this shy butterfly lives in mountain woodlands in the Northwest.

All things must change
To something new, to
something strange.

Henry Wadsworth Longfellow
(1807–1882)
American poet

And what's a butterfly?
     At best,
He's but a caterpillar, drest.

John Gay (1685–1732)
English poet and playwright

The butterfly lures us not only because he is beautiful, but because he is transitory. The caterpillar is uglier, but in him we can regard the better joy of becoming.

Cynthia Ozick, b. 1928
American writer

PAINTED LADY
Vanessa cardui

*Inhabits open spaces in temperate zones worldwide. **The** caterpillars feed on thistles and nettles.*

EASTERN
TAILED BLUE
Everes comyntas

*This small bluish-white **butterfly**
is abundant in the East.*

REGAL FRITILLARY
Speyeria idalia

*This large fritillary is limited to moist meadows **and** woodlands in the Midwest.*

BUCKEYE
Junonia coenia

This strong flier lives in American fields west of the Rockies. Adults visit plantain and figwort.

MORMON METALMARK
Apodemia mormo

Most common in the mountains of the Southwest, these colorful butterflies frequent dry, open areas.

How soft indeed the sound
Of butterflies eating!

Takayama Kyoshi (1874-1959)
Japanese poet

Even in silence, beauty is
eloquent beyond the power
of words.

Anonymous

WHITE M
HAIRSTREAK
Parrhasius m-album

A fast flier that inhabits oak forests in the South. Adults are attracted to small white flowers such as boneset.

VICEROY
Basilarchia archippus

This nonpoisonous species mimics the poisonous monarch butterfly. Viceroys are found across the U.S., usually near sources of water.

Butterflies that make sounds are not unknown. For example, male Diana butterflies audibly click their wings when disturbed. This sound is a warning to trespassers on the butterflies' territory.

CABBAGE WHITE
Pieris rapae

Widespread throughout North America. Adults are attracted to lavender.

COMMON ALPINE
Erebia epipsodea

Found from the Rockies into Alaska, this butterfly seeks damp areas, especially at higher altitudes.

WESTERN TIGER SWALLOWTAIL
Pterourus rutulus

Inhabits moist areas from British Columbia through California. Caterpillars eat willow; adults enjoy phlox and thistle.

PEARLY CRESCENTSPOT
Phyciodes tharos

Makes its home in grassy areas across North America. Adults are attracted to ageratum, thistle, and dandelions.

Small is beautiful.

Proverb

In life, as in art, the beautiful
moves in curves.

Sir Henry Bulwer (1801–1872)
English diplomat

In the lane as I came along just now I noticed one spot, ten feet square or so, where more than a hundred had collected, holding a revel, a gyration-dance, or butterfly good-time, winding and circling, down and across, but always keeping within the limits.... Butterflies and butterflies continue to flit to and fro, all sorts, white, yellow, brown, purple—now and then some gorgeous

fellow flashing lazily **by** on
the wing like artists' **palettes**
dabb'd with every color.

Walt Whitman (1819–1892)
American poet

GREAT SPANGLED
FRITILLARY
Speyeria cybele

Lives in open woodlands. The nocturnal caterpillars eat violets; the adults love thistle.

LITTLE WOOD SATYR
Megisto cymela

Inhabits moist, grassy woodlands east of the Rockies. Adults usually fly just above the grass.

GREAT PURPLE HAIRSTREAK
Atlides halesus

This butterfly's caterpillars feed on mistletoe in the lower U.S.; the adults are strong fliers.

COMMON WHITE
Pontia protodice

♂

♀

This common butterfly inhabits disturbed open areas, such as fields, throughout the U.S.

♀

DIANA
Speyeria diana

♂

This midwestern species lives in woodlands near sources of water and seeks out violets.

Everything beautiful impresses us as sufficient to itself.

Henry David Thoreau (1818–1862)
American writer

Close as they were when resting, they fairly buffeted one another in midair. . . . As if a pile of Northern autumn leaves, fallen to earth, suddenly remembered days of greenness and humming bees, and strove to raise themselves again to the bare branches overhead.

William Beebe (1877–1962)
American naturalist and explorer

Nothing is wasted—nothing lost.
The bird that thrusts against the air
Does so only at the cost
Of other wings no longer there.

John Ritchey
Twentieth-century American poet

MARINE BLUE
Leptotes marina

♂

♀

Ventures northward annually from its territory in the south-western U.S., seeking areas of new plant growth.

GULF FRITILLARY
Agraulis vanillae

Seen in open, sunny areas across the U.S. The caterpillars eat passion flowers.

LONG-TAILED SKIPPER
Urbanus proteus

Frequents river and stream banks in the southern U.S. The caterpillars eat legumes.

ACMON BLUE
Icaricia acmon

♀

♂

*Widespread in the western U.S.
The caterpillars secrete a sweet
liquid that attracts ants, which
then protect the caterpillars
from wasps.*

QUESTION MARK
Polygonia interrogationis

*Inhabits both wooded and open
areas east of the Rockies. The
adults have silver question marks
on the undersides of their hind
wings.*

COMMON SULPHUR
Colias philodice

Often found in fields and pastures, this ubiquitous species searches for clover and phlox.

For beauty being the best of
    all we know
Sums up the unsearchable and
    secret aims
Of nature.

Robert Bridges (1844–1930)
English poet

This book has been bound using
handcraft methods and Smyth-sewn
to ensure durability.

The dust jacket and interior
were illustrated by Paul Richardson
and Simon Thomas.

The dust jacket and interior
was designed by Nancy Loggins.

The text was edited by Gregory C. Aaron.

The introduction was written
by George S. Glenn, Jr.

The text was set in CG Collage,
with ITC Garamond, by Richard Conklin.